Meghdootam

Translated By:
Basanta Kumar Samanta

First Published in January 2023

ISBN: 978-93-5704-843-9

BLUEROSE PUBLISHERS

www.BlueRoseONE.com

info@bluerosepublishers.com

+91 8882 898 898

Cover Design:

Aveek

Typographic Design:

Rohit

Distributed by: BlueRose, Amazon, Flipkart

Epic of Meghdootam composed in Sanskrit
By Poet Kalidas

Preface

Iswar Chandra Vidyasagar, a scholar of Sanskrit, remarked that if the great poet Kalidas had not composed any other epic, he would still be considered the unparalleled poet of Sanskrit in India.

Kalidas was born in the third or fourth century A.D in Ujjaini, now in Madhya Pradesh, India. In his epic, Kalidas brings to life the natural world, including rivers, rivulets, hills, forests, villages, cities, trees and flowers to bring relief to Yaksha, who has been banished. He also depicts the lifeless cloud taking on the consciousness of Yaksha and running to deliver a message to Yaksha's wife. When cloud appears, the hills weep, the rivers respond, and Kalidas describes the cloud's path in vivid detail. His epic is full of beautiful descriptions, such as the sweet smell of wet soil, the beauty of the kadamba forest, and the buds of the land champa, all of which transform the reader to a dream world. Kalidas did not set a specific precedent for future poets; instead he was immersed in his own world of genuine creativity. His epic is described as "eyes becoming pleasant upon seeing, hearts becoming happy, the world becoming a happier abode, a stream of honey pouring into the ears, drawing out the heart like honey." It is a peerless work.

In Raghubangsha epic, Kalidas has said, "at the end of yoga I shall leave my body. When my body becomes old, through yoga like torn clothes, it can be thrown out and then achieve a new body." So this yoga was in vogue at the time of Kalidas. It is presumed that great poet Kalidas practised "yoga" which helped him know and analyse mind of matter as well as humans and non-humans, thus success came to him.

Contents

Part 1

Meghdootam
Cloud On The East

Stanza 1

King of Alaka, Kuber's servant, Yaksha, due to indecent love for his wife failed to discharge his normal duty, for that reasons Kuber had cursed the servant, saying that, losing all magical power as Yaksha, you will have to spend life for one year at Ramgiri hills like an ordinary man. Ramgiri is also place of pilgrimage. In the past God Ram and His wife, Sita lived on that hill constructing a hut. Now all places there become holy, as daughter of Janak (wife of God Ram) had taken bath in the pond and all the places are soothing under shades of leaves of trees. So, by any standard the place is not bad for living.

Stanza 2

Yaksha has been without the company of his beloved partner for eight months and still has four more months to go. As a result, his once robust body has become thin and lean, and he has unknowingly lost his golden bangels. One day, during the rainy season of Ashad, Yaksha sees a new cloud in the sky that resembles a wild elephant. Captivated by this majestic sight, he sits motionless, mesmerized by the cloud's playful movements.

Stanza 3

As a servant of the king of Alaka, Yaksha has been separated from his beloved wife for a long time and is filled with pain as he watches the new cloud. Despite trying to supress his emotions, his mind is filled with thoughts. His life has been turned upside down. In whose heart there is no dearth of anything, in the heat of sorrow of separation from beloved person, whose life is not burnt to ashes – Man of mind who is not even for a moment does not go out of sight from eyes, such happy people also become mad seeing new cloud. Despite having all, he feels, something is missing from him, his life becomes restless. His life becomes on the other hand, for this hapless man, neck to neck love in the matter of marriage, it is going away – far away – my mental condition is so unbearable and terrible, is it required to tell you?

Stanza 4

Gradually, month of shravan second month of rainy seasons became thick with clouds. Yaksha who is in separation from wife comparing his physical condition and understood that his beloved wife in separation from him may not survive, she may even die in unbearable condition with advent of new rainy season. I did not die – we will come together – this message, if it was at least sent to her, she might have been alive, so being mad, Yaksha thought to send message to cloud to communicate to his beloved better half , he welcomed cloud heartily and graciously decorated with kuruchi flowers which blossom in rainy season.

Stanza 5

Where is the lifeless cloud, produced in mixing of smoke, light, water and wind, these four maters? Where are living humans having all senses, who can go from this place to faraway place to deliver message? – how far it will be possible to send messages at Alaka , so much far away , distressed Yaksha could not think at all , or who are obsessed with sexual desire , they lose their sense to judge between life having consciousness and matter without life. They behave like this –

They have no sense right or wrong. Do not abide by honour dishonour.

Stanza 6

Yaksha invoked birth of cloud in a famous family. Oh, cloud! I know you are the descendent of world famous Puskar Abartak Lake Cloud, above all, you are the chief force and right hand of Indra, the king of heaven. Your power is unlimited, any time you can change your colour. Thinking all aspects I appear before you like a beggar. As misfortune engulfs me, I am here today. The main strength of my family – of my heart who is my better half, she is living alone far away. Cloud if begging to a person of high grade like you fails, that is also better to me than to have success from others, who are small, very small, that is not desirable, in that achievement mind becomes low.

Stanza 7

Cloud you have the power to bring relief to those suffering from heat. I am burning with the pain of separation from my partner, who is also suffering from being separated from me. We have been cursed by Kuber, the owner of vast wealth and there seems to be no way to remedy this or to be reunited with my beloved. If you could kindly carry a message to my partner, it may bring us both some relief. Please visit Alaka at least once. It is a renowned place of pilgrimage, home to Kuber and his vast wealth, and the sight of it brings joy to the eyes and mind. Additionally, the god Shiva resides in the gardens outside Alakapuri where the moon's stainless light reflects off his large body onto the white palaces and houses, all of which are as white as ice and beautiful to behold.

There is no place more pious and satisfying than this.

Stanza 8
Cloud,

you bring hope to those in distress by easing their pains. Did you know that you are the centre of hope for women whose husbands are far away? When they see you flying in the sky, they are filled with hope that their husbands are returning home, and they run to look at you imagining all sorts of things. They are in separation from their husbands, and have not combed their hairs or applied oil. As they look up at you, their unkempt hairs fall on faces, obstructing their view. They cannot clearly see you or fulfil their desires, but they keep their hairs in place with their hands as they gaze at you. From above, you will see a group of faces with necks like lotus moons, each one blossoming at a rate of 16 aanas (hundred percent). These faces will be especially beautiful as they hope that this time you will bring their husbands home. Cloud! There is no one as confined as me, stuck in a distant place when you appear.

Stanza 9
Brother,

Today is the gracious day, also auspicious moment for journey. Behold how rainy wind is blowing from the south to the north to which direction you will go, wind is blowing in the direction, so wind is in your favour. Again, look at your left, being pleasant chatak birds (swallow birds) are singing nicely, this is no mean bad sign. Again this time when you are moving in the sky, then like previous occasion, cluster of long – necked wading birds desiring for copulation will fall on you, they will render cordial service to you, because they know, they cannot get opportunity for copulation without cover of your veil, though available, it is not suitable. So I am telling auspicious moment for journey has come, do not loose time without cause, start your journey.

Stanza 10
Cloud!

Why you are not responding? What are you thinking? Reaching far away at Alaka you may not see her? Are you thinking? I am telling, you will very much see her. She is the only wife of her husband - her husband also has only wife, both are closely dependent on each other. Had I five wives, my separation did not affect much. That I am her only husband, she better knows. Can see abandon hope for me? On reaching, you will see, she has not fallen in danger, did not die. Can she die? She is living with hope for me, to die is impossible for her. Going there, you will see that, still she is counting, how many days are left to one year of curse – she is counting that. That wife – your elder brother's wife, if you go quickly now, surely you will see her. But stormy rains are in your front, if you delay on that way or fumble on your judgement, then perhaps- she will die during those days – till now she is alive strengthening her heart. Wish for union is a big hope. In that hope, soft heart of woman dreams as long as the flower is attached to the stalk.

The heart breathes, and hopes; as soon as hope comes to end, life dries like flower attached to dry stalks. So, do not delay.

Stanza 11
Brother,

You still remain silent you have to go above – are you perplexed? is it not? You will not have paucity of companion on the way, they will serve you, will please you from any side which they will find comfortable, you too know, in rainy season, ganders do not stay in this region. They fly to manas sarover which is situated near our residence. Among birds, among drakes in beauty, quality, walking, chirping, they are kings so their names are ganders. They will accompany you, each with a piece of white lotus in their mouth. You are dark-skinned, and beneath you a flock of white geese. The sight of the stainless white lotus in their red lips is beautiful. It's a marvel! They will be your only companions on your journey to Kailash. Don't think negatively. With your thundering, mind and heart, everything becomes pleasant. From your thunder, bhukundali flowers crack the earth and tremble as they raise their heads announcing that the earth will be abundant with bumper crops. The lives of the geese are restless with the desire to go to Kailash and they will be your trusted companions. So what are you waiting for? Start you journey now brother.

Stanza 12
Brother,

Why are you delaying? Start now. Your long-time friend, who is a true friend in every sense, is waiting for you to take leave by embracing the hill. If you embrace the hill at the beginning of your journey, your mind will be fulfilled because every stone of the hill bears the holy dust and footprints of God Ramachandra who is worshipped by Trilok (heaven, earth and the infernal world). Is there any other hill as fortunate? When you embrace the hill after the long summer's heat, you will see that the hill's body releases a vapor of suffering from the long separation. The entire body of the hill will be covered in drops of cold water.

Brother, that is not water, but rather the tears of joy and pleasure in the hill's heart at seeing you again. You have such a dear friend at your departure, so why be afraid to embrace him at least once before you go? Now, start your journey, brother.

Stanza 13
Cloud!

What are you thinking? Which way you will have to go? Acquaintance and address of the path (road) on which you will go – all I am telling in details, listen with attention, take it into your heart. "for your going" I told, but why? Do you know? You are now cloud of new rainy season, full of water; you will have to go judging so many things carefully; you will not be able to rise high like thin, light waterless cloud, moreover, from this place you will not be able to go to Alaka straightway. You will have to undertake journey in a zigzag way. So many mountains and hills will come on your way, somewhere avoiding, you will have to move forward keeping right to left . I know all intricacies that I am telling, hear my descriptions of the way so that you can go. Brother, then the message which is to be given to my beloved better half, hear that. I am surely telling; it will pass through your inner mind.

Brother, whenever feel tired, you cannot move further then on that way; resting for a while from hill to hill you will be able to go otherwise, you will release your water. Again, if you feel that you are light to some extent wind may fly you elsewhere, instantly drinking very transparent and very light water of streams from the hill will strengthen your body.

Stanza14
Cloud,

Hear me. In these hilly regions reside many Siddhas practising yoga along with their families. From these places you turn straight to the north, you will fly in the sky. Behold down, how bushes of beautiful canes are arranged in orderly manner, as if somebody has painted and kept here. From these rows of bushes of canes suddenly seeing you flying in the sky simple minded female Siddhas, wives of Siddhas who practice yoga, will look at your unexpected activities with curiosity widening their eyes, thinking whether any storm is winding up from behind the peak of the hill. They are too naive to think that stone cannot fly- they have no minimum knowledge about it. They will tremble from fear that snakes present all around will come to fight with you. Do not look at them. It is not prudent to quarrel on the way. You will go avoiding them. Otherwise, if you get involved in this matter, you will be badly delayed on the way. Do not do that. My gracious friend.

Stanza15
Cloud!

Look at the front, indradhanush is rising, slowly from the heap of soil of white ants that have grown on the upper layer of the hill, reflecting various colours of ornament like red, blue, green, yellow. It is a pleasure to see. If you move to the north, some portion of indradhanush will be touched on the southern side of your head. How it will be looking more attractive! When dark coloured Shyam, God Krishna dressed as Gopal with mind-blowing feathers of peacock placed on his head bending slightly looks highly attractive, likewise, your dark body will also be looking beautiful.

Stanza16
Brother,

Output of agricultural work from hard toil at the cost of life throughout the year depends only on your hand, all efforts become fruitless if you do not discharge rains in the season. Who does not know this system? So, when you will appear today then, simple wives of farmers will look at you with hope, their husbands' entire labour becomes successful by your kindness. These rural wives will look at you with affectionate and pleasant eyes, they will see you. Their hopes will not come to end.

Brother,

There is no crookedness in their eyes, there is no luxury, there is no fashion, there is no desire in eyes. In that looking there is no dancing of rolling eyebrows to tempt mind of males, they have no alluring gestures. In that you will get only simplicity, only love and you will get only divine love, love without temptation, only "amrita" (honey), stainless moon light, holy brightness like flower. When you will see their attraction in eyes, you will think that those rural beautiful women have, as if, drunk you through their eyes. How fortunate you are. Thus, going there, you will rise above the tilled land. That tilled land on the slopes of the hill is already hot in the extreme heat of summer, whenever, a spell of light rain from you will fall on that land, then from that hot land how nice wet flavour will rise, all the places around the tilled land will be swayed in that flavour. Smelling that nice wet flavour, moving forward a little bit, then turning to the west on a short distance, then again to the north, you will go quickly.

Stanza17
Brother,

Moving up over the plateau crawling you will have serious trouble, no doubt, but for that you need not worry. When you will go up, you will see at first in your front the hill namely, Amrakut (hill of mango tree). Look at that hill. How the hill remains high rising its head before you reach, as if it is seeing how far you are. The hill is very much indebted to you. When ancestral forests were being burnt in wild fire, then only you were there; you discharged rain water and extinguished that terrible fire of hot summer. Nobody went there. Can the hill forget you? Today, when you will be tired from journey, that Amrakut hill will lessen your trouble keeping you on its head. He, who is even low-minded does not refuse shelter to his friend who has rendered good service to him, on the contrary, Amrakut hill is very tall in comparison. The hill will be grateful giving you shelter, is there any doubt?

Stanza 18
Brother,

What I tell about Amrakut hill is that it is called by that name as its top is full of mango trees. The top of the hill looks like monastery or a temple comprising of sweet sugar like cone of the banana rising in the sky. No other hill is so high. That is only one. It has risen high piercing through sky. Mango trees have grown around the hill and ripe mangoes are hanging from the branches. The top of the hill resembling monastery is turned into pale shade of light from the pale colour of mangoes.

Cloud!

Your colour is as black as braid of hair, rubbed with oil. When you will sit on the pale top of the hill, beautiful goddesses will look down at you from the sky and you will be thrilled watching them. All around prevails colour and at the stalk there is dark colour, from above goddesses will enjoy keenly nice natural image of magnificent beauty.

Stanza 19
Brother,

There are so many groves on the Amrakut hill. These groves are platforms with full of thick trees and plants. In those groves, created by Goddess of nature in her own hand, simple forest dwellers like kol, bhil, santhal come with their family enjoy pleasure. Those places are very attractive. In the heat of summer those groves might have been put to trouble. After a short rest, discharging small quantity of rainwater, becoming light, you will go some distance quickly. Going there you will see the river, Narmada. In the summer it is flowing slowly with small quantity of water on the slopes on the Vindhya hill. If you see her thin body comprising of many streams, it will strike your heart, you may burst into tears also. You will discharge some water there. Slopes of the vast Vindhya hill are full of stones - big and small, high and low; through those bumpy roads, streams of the hill are flowing in hundreds and thousands in irregular way, reaching the plain being merged into one and finally converged with river. Seeing Narmada, it seems that gracious wife falling on the ugly feet of her arrogant, humourless, heartless husband, is becoming restless and weeping endlessly. Her colour of body becomes pale from hundreds of streams coming from the body of dark Vindhya hill, surrounded by forests. The streams are falling on river Narmada; from high sky downward, you will see red, yellow reddish, somewhere white line of that stream. It will look like image of a trunk of a big elephant decorated with vermillion, sandal, eye salve.

Stanza 20

Oh! How beautiful is that place. In groves of jambu trees streams are rustling and jumping with bubbling sound. Debris of water are sieved by the roots and branches of jambu tree like scoop net; streams of pure and stainless water are flowing, whatever, poison water has will be removed; after cleaning this water becomes sweet to forest elephants of the Vindhya hill. Other water mixed with camphor does not match with this sweet water.

Cloud! You will discharge there. But after rain, you drink that roaming sweet water. Ayurveda (medical guidance, prescribed in Atharva Veda, written by sages of ancient India) says that such water strengthens broad body. You may feel sick from long journey from Ramgad hill. So, you spewed from your stomach, you will be light, then you drink water, as prescribed in medical guidelines, as a result, you will not shiver from illness. Moreover, if you do not fill your stomach after spewing then wind will move you at any direction. If there is nothing inside, the wind will take you away like cotton. It is not only you, the one whose inside is empty becomes very light his woe has no end. The one whose inside is heavy has importance everywhere. He does not stand up and sit down with the help of others.

Stanza21
Cloud!

Wherever you go, pomp and grandeur will be on that way. As if, king of kings, called by name "chakravarty" has gone and his used and decorated clothes have fallen on that way. With your new rains of the year so many kadam flowers will blossom on the kadam trees; the ones which are about to blossom will blossom at any moment. How many days will be required if spray of new water touches them? A wonderful image will grow of the blossoms; the pollen tubes will give a hue of green and pale colour. Again, in wet and damp places, land champas will rise with buds in their mouths. When rain falls, they are seen and their flowers blossom. Again, in the extreme heat, the groves of trees got burnt extremely. Soil surface was turned to chasm. With your discharged sweet water, how sweet flavour is coming out from that wet soil and it will madden all around. In the heat of summer, tired male and female deer's after becoming cold with your discharge of water will look at the beauty of the kadamba forest. The deer will look up, again their faces keeping downward, chewing those buds of land champa, smelling that wet flavour will get maddened and will run on your rain soaked path, as if, they will show the world that this way that cloud which bears pleasure of the world, has gone. How fortunate you are.

Stanza22
Brother,

For my beloved better-half, that you will go quickly, there is no doubt. But still, I am seeing you being late for a considerable period reaching every hill. Because, I know, you love kurchi flower very much on those hills. The hills remain white with innumerable kuruchi flowers under new rainy season; the flavour spreads to all ten sides of the hill and is being enjoyed. Can you reach there without delay? Then again, seeing your beautiful body emerged from new water of rains those peacocks who love you with their lives will dance raising their plumages and with their white watery eyes mingled with pleasure will see you raising their blue throat. When they will accept you with sweet calls, will you be able to reach their quickly ignoring calls of their lives? Never it be. Your heart is very soft, even who has ruthless and humourless heart cannot go avoiding their lovely calls.

Stanza23
Cloud!

Going in the land of ten headed man named Ravana of the epic, Ramayana, have you even thought what of his magnificent beauty will emerge? From the beginning, the ganders taking stalks of lotuses in their mouth were going to Manas Sarovar with you. When you will go to the land of the ten headed Ravana, those ganders will stay there for some days, afterwards, they will fly with you. The land of ten headed Ravana is surrounded by rows of jambu trees, outside the row it is again surrounded by ketaki trees. Inside exists beautiful garden; such nice land, full of gardens, you will find nowhere such garden in India. As you reach, buds of flowers will blossom on ketaki, some white thorns of flowers will come out, as if , on seeing you, queen of garden has risen wrapping her entire body with thorns. Inside the boundary of white ketaki flowers jambu trees are standing in rows, and in those trees ripe and innumerable jambu fruits like bluish diamond are hanging. You look from above and imagine. Even thinking of that magnificent scene brings tremendous pleasure to heart. Then again, in the villages, along the roads, so many tall trees are standing thinking of advent of rains. So many rural birds like crows have begun to prepare nests in those trees, moreover, with their hue and cry, entire village is roaring in sound. How beautiful the scene is.

Stanza24
Brother cloud!

Going to Vidisha, world famous capital of ten headed Ravana you will fulfill all lovable desires of your heart. Because, such city of enjoyment is not existing anywhere. That the hill, river, named vetravati being struck by the pebbles is running gleefully in yellow colour and being thrashed by stones on the shores with roaring sound. Going there you drink some of that wavy water. You will think that, being unable to bear torture by the ten headed Ravana the river, vetravati, personified as woman, is requesting through shuddering her eyes not to proceed further. So her expressed sweet sound is coming out through murmuring sound. Getting you so near whole body of vetravati has become red in love. Her body turns so much red- coloured because it is colour of red soil.

Brother how you are fortunate?

Stanza25

To stay there you have no problem. At the fringe area of that city, mind blowing hill exists. On that hill sitting, take rest for a while. On the hill innumerable kadam flowers are blossomed. Seeing, it will seem, as if his entire body becomes thrilled meeting a friend like you after a long time. On the slopes of that hill many caves exist; many rooms of stones exist from cutting by chisel and constructed by hand. At that time, perhaps, so many sages used to stay there. Now those remain vacant. But those caves remain completely vacant, that cannot be said. So, many illicit male lovers of the city go to enjoy with females in pairs, loveable women of the city go with decorated cloths. In the solitary hilly caves enjoying with them returns to their houses. Moreover, those caves become full with sweet smell of their body and flavour of blossomed flowers, pressed under their bodies; some times in stormy wind that flavour coming out tell the world that how the sexual desire of males of vidisha city monstrous, that cannot be checked at all.

Stanza26

Do you know, why name of the hill is "downhill?" Truly, this is not very high. Whenever heart desires, handsome males of the city rush there. So, sitting on the hill whatever you can, remove tiredness, afterwards, you will run again. The river, vetravati is running down, you are running from the sky into that river. On both sides of the river there are gardens of flowers, in the groves there are crores and crores of jasmine flowers blossomed. It looks as if two sides of the river is decorated with flavour and bright cloth of silk. Through that background of forest and river, vertebrate is running speedily and chirpingly. Again, in those gardens of jasmine flower women of same age have come in groups to pluck flowers with small basket in their hands. Plucking, moving unfolding their hearts, speaking their words of mind in those male less gardens. In the heat of sun perspiration is falling on their necks, again and again, with their hands, they are erasing that perspiration which is falling on their necks; unmindfully, hands are touching lotuses attached to ears. Lotuses are pressed and thrashed. Brother, discharging a spell of water on jasmine flowers in those gardens of jasmine you will see suddenly that your shadow is falling down. The heat of the sun becomes less, those flowers pluckers in thousands raising their heads are looking at you for a while, like familiar old friend, they are seeing with heartfelt love.

Stanza27
Cloud!

Ending your enjoyment at vidisha you are going to the north. But do not go to the north straight in that way. Turning to the south-west to some extent, you will have to go after seeing Ujjayini. It's top of high rising palace when seen, seems that the city is waiting for somebody.

Brother, after sitting there you go. Whoever invites you cordially, you cannot refuse that invitation. How women of Ujjayini have rectangular eyes and oscillating body, if you do not see that electrifying, shivering and bright eyes, then your life becomes futile; promise me, you will go, otherwise, you will fall in sin of self-deception.

Stanza28
Brother,

For going to Ujjayini, situated at south-west part of Vidisha, as soon as you will start, slightly move forward, then at the west you will face the river, Nirvindhya. Originating from the river, Vindhya, this hilly river is running on the way towards north. Very often, ditch of the river is full of heaps of stones, large pebbles, sometimes clean ditch. So, the river, thrashed by stones, is flowing in roaring sound, sometimes, on the contrary, it is flowing quietly. Where there is obstruction, in that place water is whirling in a big way. For a while being restless, speed is splited due to obstruction by heavy stones; Nirvindhya's quiet movement pushes her by whopping on such stones, and in the next moment flowing calmly like a nice river. From above seeing large whirling motion of water, it seems that nice river, Nirvindhya seeing is running with you heartily. Above you are running, down on land such beautiful river is running, thrashed by stones against her legs falling down suddenly again rising and running. Sometimes, somewhere after falling down she cannot rise. Looking at you she has fallen. Being busy with emotion playing in her mind her sense of shame has gone away. Moreover, like whirlpool, her deep belly-bottom is being seen. Further, being thrashed by stone water is running with bubbling sound, common swams are trying to come upstream swimming, in the force of water current their rows are being shattered and thrown aside. Swams are calling; that sound of water mixing with swams' call is producing wonderful sweet sound like rattling sound of chandrahar (pendant).

Brother! At least come down, after enjoying beauty, you go. Besides expressing this emotion, they cannot tell. Do not deprive the river, Nirvindhya. In long heat, this thin body that Nirvindhya retains, it is better, you go shedding rain water. What is necessary of picking curse of others?

Staza29
Cloud!

No one is fortunate like you. You will appear in the sky, you will be seen, with this hope, so many rivers are lying, do you not think that? In the extreme heat, or in separation, how they have become thin and pale; they have dried and turned into a braid of hair, with hope for seeing you. Still rivers are flowing with scanty water, but, they did not die. Going there, you shed rain water, then and then, automatically their sufferings will be removed and will be alive. How many people are so fortunate? Sindhu river originating from Vindhya hill is going to the east;

woeful Sindhu river, which is so much dried up is lying like a long braid of hair; braid of hair gradually becomes thin to thinner, likewise, thin bodied Sindhu is turning gradually from thin to thin, ultimately vanishes. Yellow leaves from trees from both sides of the river are falling on the river, they have made water pale; it seems that, in separation, blood being dried is also looking pale. Are you less fortunate? How many persons spend such sweet days of separation from you? Try to remove such worst condition of Sindhu, only you do who is so compassionate of the river, Sindhu.

Stanza30
Brother,

Then you will reach Avanti. In that place "Advutartha Brihatkatha" is in great publicity. The olds in the locality are engaged in gossiping, day and night on kidnapping of the beloved daughter of Pradyot by Vatsaraj Udayan. In the light of social ethics, so many fictitious stories are always discussed. I have already told you earlier, you will sit for a moment at the outskirts of Ujjayini.

Cloud!

Capitals of Avanti, is called Ujjayini or Vishala. That city by name is Vishala. Similarly, in wealth, in beauty, in all respects, it is rightfully Vishala Ujjayini. In self-pride, it is victorious as it is on the top of all. Looking at the city it seems, there is no other such beautiful city on earth; cannot be built at all. All those great men, who have gone to heaven, so have again come back to earth and at the time of coming, have taken with them some portion of remaining piety of heaven. That small quantity of piety so achieved, is showering brightness as bright as stainless white to this magnificent city Vishala or Ujjayini on the soil of earth.

Stanza31
Brother!

What shall I tell about that Vishala? There everything is magnificent. In the morning, pleasant cold wind blows from waves of river, Shipra which is flowing slowly. The water is touched by bodies of women, who are tired of sufferings in their bodies and the wind removes all tiredness of women. Loose body becomes thrilled again with touch of that wind. Does morning wind have any other in parallel? In the river Shipra lakhs and lakhs lotus flower blossom fully or are yet to blossom. Wind blowing in the forest of lotuses is smelling flavour of lotus flowers and playing hide and seek with them. In the cold morning wind, storks are blowing sweet sound and floating. The sound enters the ears of women, who are neither sleeping, nor awaken. Breaking insensitiveness of sleep, they are immersed in another magnificent still world. Their body and mind, as if, got thrilled in a dreamy way. As if, submissive dearest one is moving his hand slowly and slowly on the body of his tired beloved woman telling so many sweet words. He is appeasing. He is doing penance for his fault.

Stanza32
Friend!

To remove distress in separation of sindhu, you have to make your body light. For that you need not be afraid. Whatever trouble you had suffered, that you will take care of, by blessings of goddess, Vishalakshi of Vishala. The well-dressed women lighting candle smear the smell of candle in their hairs; hairs become scented. Mixing with smell of hair, flavour comes out through window. As soon as you go there, that nice smell of the candle will touch your body; from its touch, to speak the truth, your body will expand. As if, your body will transform into new one. Your limbs will be strengthened. All the distress of the body will be removed. There pet peacocks seeing you will welcome you, dancing and raising their plumages; you are their friend, very intimate to their hearts. There stand many tall wonderful palaces. In those palaces, beautiful women dressed with flower are always welcoming. Women are wandering wearing garland of flowers, armlets of flowers and a neckless of flowers. In cottages of the palace, flavour of flowers is spreading all around. That ground floor of the palace has been painted so nicely with lac-dye, it seems as if the lime is smeared round the feet of women like flowers. Brother seeing this magnificent beauty from sitting atop the palace for a while, remove some of your pain as suffered on the way. Not only your pain will be removed, but eyes will also enjoy that pleasure.

Stanza33
Cloud!

Going to Ujjayani, you will once see the temple of Trijagat Guru, Chandalika Pati, God Mahadev on the shore of river, Gandhavati. Your complexion is just like the colour of neck of Nilkantha. So his followers will look at you without blink of eye and with much affection, they will gaze at you. Are you less fortunate?

Brother! I am not telling for achieving piety; going there, your heart will also get soothed. Beside the temple of mahakal Mahadev, a wonderful garden is situated. Pleasant cold wind is blowing from the river, Gandhavati, to that garden of flowers; flavour of flowers is pervading all around. Even has that any parallel? You will enjoy such wind. In water of Gandhavati innumerable lotus flowers blossom. Young women play water game rubbing various scented oil; for that matter water of river always become scented with their scent of bodies. Wind blows, which brings flavour of lotus with scent of bodies of beautiful women; wind blows which shudders trees blossomed with flowers in the forest. Now think at least once, how that place is so charming and enjoyable. Seeing the temple there you move forward.

Stanza34
Friend,

Except the time of act of greeting god, Mahakal, by waving a lamp, don't you spend time there. You wait for some time, until the sun sets in the west. In the evening, act of greeting Mahakal will be performed, that you brother, if roar in thunder, then it will not be necessary to beat drum. Your roaring will act like beating of drum. Then and then your roaring will be successful. You will readily achieve piety for serving god. Rendering satisfactory service to God Mahakal, you go from there. If He is annoyed, no protection is available to you, mind it. He seems to be forgetful God (Bholanath), he always carries in the hand of that Tripurari the most dreadful weapon, Trishul. Is there any necessity to irritate such God to be angry?

Stanza35

In that temple in the evening, at the time of act of greeting God Mahakal, "devadashis" (prostitutes), are coming well-dressed and winding fly-brush while dancing. Their legs step in musical rhythm during beating of drums for act of greeting Mahakal; the moon shaped ring tied with waist makes wonderful sweet sound ringing in ears. Entire hands are decorated with bejewelled ornament. How pleasant it is, when its brightness touches the handle of fly-brush then how glittering it is to enjoy. Beautiful women's soft hands like lotus flowers winding fly-brush become gradually loose due to idleness. Do those soft hands exist now? These hands have been scratched by nails of their cruel lovers. In the heat through the day, their wounds have become dry and feeling very uneasy.

Brother, that time if you discharge two or four drops of new rain water on those wounds, then their pain will lesson very much and they will also look at you through curved eyes, thinking, "Who is such lovely friend". Every time their curved eyes look at you, the black stars of black eyes will come at slight angle and see you, as if, bubble bees are flying from their lotus eyes to you and they will again wind their fly-brushes. They do not have the courage to look at you in still eyes. Their profession has no social recognition, moreover, it is the temple of God, they may face condemnation, for that, they will not look at you frequently. In this way within a moment from their eyes innumerable bubbles will run to you in rows. Once you think, fortune is yours.

Stanza36
Brother,

In this temple, you have to perform further a small work. Task is not such big one, but result of that is far reaching. By the curse of a sage Nrada in ancient times, one famous king Gajashur obtained mouth of elephant and became famous. Afterwards, killing Gajashur, Rudradev takes skin, which is blood stained. Bholanath (Mahesh) loves such blood-stained skin. Whenever god Shiva (Bholanath) starts frantic dance at the time of annihilation of world, blood-stained large bodied Mahadev would raise His hands like white monument many times, as he desires that blood-stained skin of Gajanan; then and then His attendants bringing that skin would keep His hands. Shiva taking that skin would tremble the world by dancing continuously, and at the end gradually becomes calm. When frantic dance is started in full rhythm, none can stop that dance except his own wish. This is not a dance brother, as if, it is universal dissolution. Daughter of the king of mountain, Uma feels pain seeing, three eyed God, Shiva tired for dancing. Uma obtained Shiva through religious austerities. She is a daughter of Daksha, wife of Shiva, a chest or a faithful wife. In the evening when performance of winding by fly-brush before God Mahadeva is over, when Chandrashekhar (Shiva) will start dancing, then within a very short duration if you fall on hands of god Shiva and discharge two or one drops of water Chandrashekhar will stop dancing. You will be like jaba (hibiscus) flower, catching your evening red colour and

Chandrashekhar will stop dancing then thinking you as blood- stained skin of snake, dance will not continue further. Uma's heart becomes quiet, she will be satisfied. In unwavering eye seeing your devotion to Shiva she will bless you. Brother, do not miss this opportunity.

Stanza37
Friend!

You have to do the task a little bit at Ujjayni. At night when king's way is covered with darkness and so deep that even a needle cannot penetrate, not to speak of viewing with eyes. It is a love tryst of a lover. Women are going to assignation for love with males covering their body with blue dress, walking slowly and silently to their desired places. Night is dark, sometimes, they stumble, and sometimes they fall, troubles increase. At that time with a little break, without making any sound, without any hue and cry, you tell your lighting to dazzle on you, so that, it remains attached with your deep black body, like golden line on rough stone glittering for a while; resultantly in that light they will see the way. Already they are going on the wrong way in darkness, if they see light, they can see that way to some extent. That time, you do not discharge water of rain or roar in thunder. They are always petrified; they have no end of fears. If you run after them, they will die. Promise to me, do not hammer with a scimitar on the body which is already lifeless.

Stanza38
Brother,

Thus, again and again, moving inside and outside, showing light, your better-half the beautiful lighting will be tired- there is no doubt. So, sitting on any high-rise palace spend the night. Your moonlight will get rest. So, you will be able to refresh tired moonlight again. That you will get the evidence that there is no sound of men from the pigeons sleeping in flocks without any sensation. If there is any sound of man, can they sleep in such deep sleep? So, spend the night on the roofs of high rise building, then your moon light may take rest for a short period. On those roofs there is no sign of people. So, without hindrance, you will be able to get your moonlight afreshed. Do not delay much at same place. Cloud, no saint man, accepting the task of a friend does not delay. Complete quickly.

Stanza39
Cloud!

In that very early morning before sun rays, debauched males return home spending whole night at another place, and are going to wives of chastity who all are idle bodies. The males console them telling false stories in seven-five different variation, they erase tears of eyes of rueful wives. So, in the morning you do not obstruct the way of sun. If you do, then those males will further delay thinking, "darkness of night is yet to end". They have no mercy and kindness at all. Else, doing that, Sun God will also be angry with you seriously. He is also not less powerful. There is no trace of it where males spent time whole night. Here Nalini becomes reddish weeping and weeping, her entire body becomes motionless and eyes brim full with tears. Sun God is moving in the morning to cool her to erase dew water by moving his hands. If you at this time suppress the hands of Sun, he will be very aggrieved. Brother, He is Sun-God. It may happen to grow from small to large. You may see what is my wretched condition. He is not God, but Kuber, whose position is much lower at the ladder; he cursed me what is the consequence? On the other hand, sun is Sabitri deva. Who is visible.

Stanza40
Brother,

Going fast, you will be gainer, not looser. Going a little bit, you will see Gamvira River. How water is clean and in happy mood with affectionate heart. Cloud! You are fortunate. What a natural beauty you have, which beautiful women do not desire? In transparent water like unblemished heart of Gamvira, your shadow will be reflected. You will be able to enter into that heart through your shadow. Your black shadow when falls on the chest of Gamvira, restless very white tiny fishes will be jumping. Normally they are white, they will look more white in black shadow. It will seem, as if, Gamvira seen you after many days is kicking continuously. Now it becomes silent. It is casting white side glance like white Kumud flowers to you. Cloud, you spray water at this moment. On the contrary, maintaining your usual image of gravity, do not spoil her such oblique glances.

Stanza41
Cloud!

In the extreme heat of summer, like other rivers, water level of Gamvira also comes down to a great extent – from the shore far down inside the ditch; height of the stream has fallen, moreover heaps of sands have risen above, along the two sides of stream. From the peak of the hill, blue cane creepers coming down the shore are hanging and bending, moving by motion of stream. Looking from above, you will see, as if, the river Gamvira personified as an actress, wearing blue cloth in the form of water which got displaced from her waist and she is catching by two hands trying to place in the proper position. You, stretched body, go as quickly leaving such uncovered loins of women. Going from there will not be easy for you. Because, any humorous person cannot go suddenly ignoring such uncovered loin of woman.

Stanza42
Brother,

Crossing Gamvira, you will have to go to Devagiri. Going a short distance on that way your all distress will be removed. Receiving your first rain-water, a hue and cry will be sounded from earth. It has suffered in the severe heat of summer generated from drying soil; your deep smell of rain water will spread all around. On the hill, cold wind is blowing with murmuring sound and in that smell, all are swayed. Big elephants with long tasks, who have so long suffered in heat of summer, are drawing wind through trunks today. The smelling of cold wind not only soothes surface of body but inside as well. Through nostrils of trunks wind is entering with loud sound. All around Dumur forest, the touch of that cold wind of new rains will ripen the fruits "Dumur"; sweet smell will spread over all directions. The cold wind rubbing all that scent on its body coming to you will render service to you. Your Gamvira will generate new strength on your depressed mind and on your body which got tired from high enjoyment.

Stanza 43
Cloud!

At that Devagiri, commander of army of Debendra, Kartick remains seated forever. He is glamourous and powerful also. Nobody can defeat him. In order to protect army of Debendra who has been defeated many times by Asura, Balandu Shekhar (husband of Parvati) through his divine power in the fire place gave birth to Kartick. He assumed the position of commander of army of Debendra. Even power of Sun God is also unmatched with him. So, brother there you have to perform a little task. You are Kamrup, prone to take image, as you like. And assume image in that fashion. Going that place, you take up the image of cloud of flower completely. Now, you are cloud of water, you discharge water of rains. Then you will be cloud of flower, you will discharge flowers. Then immersing in water of akash-Ganga, cloud, at least once, with full heart, discharging those flowers in countless streams, you will bathe Deb commander in chief, son of Parvati (wife of Shiva) by soaking cloth in water.

Stanza 44

With this you will have to do a further task at that Devagiri. At first, rendering service to Kartick Dev, as usual, you will roar, with some sound with thunder. That roaring sound whenever goes through caves will be resounded. So, it will be doubled. You will see, Kartick Deva's conveyance peacock raising its plumage will start dancing. Seeing dancing of own's conveyance, which master will not be pleased? Skanda Dev will also be enjoying that peacock is no lesser one. Son Kartick loves riding on the peacock as he used to wander. Mother Bhavani, Uma, daughter of the king of the mountain, also sees the peacock with passionate eye. If at any time, peacock's one feather gets detached, mother, then and then, will run and pick up that feather painted as chandrak, carrying stalk of lotus, she wears on her ear. She never detaches any feather by her hand; whatever gets detached falls on its own. It is no less a pleasant gesture. Father of Kartick, God Shiva, does not leave the peacock out of his view, whenever peacock goes, he always stares at him. As a result, white moonlight coming for four-head of Shiva falls on the face of peacock and its eyes become white and glittering. Do not ignore the lovely peacock of Hara-Parvati. You move forward encouraging peacock's dancing.

Stanza 45
Cloud,

Worshiping Kartick Dev in the manner, as you have done before you will move forward. Wonderful scenes will appear on your way. You will see, in the sky "Sidhas" and their wives, in pairs are playing "Vina", singing songs and are wondering. You are running. Seeing you, quickly they will move away from your path. They are afraid, if you touch with your drop of water favourite "vinas" may lose sweet sound. Then you will see on the surface, Chambal River is flowing speedily. Brother, that is not a river, but it describes the fame of king Rantidev whose glorious achievement river, Chambal is carrying. King Rantidev performing Gomedhyagana killed cows of Kamdhenu Suravi. Blood is coming out of skin of dead cows that is flowing in the form of stream. Do not forget to keep his honour. You come down a little bit and touch his holy water.

Stanza 46
Brother,

From far away, from far above, the river Charmavati is looking like a bunch of white stings, its stream is not thin but thick, very wide. From above it looks like that. Thrashing pebbles, it is running with loud sound. Heaps of white foam being deposited on stone which have covered white stream. From above, it seems, as if a garland of diamond is lying. Oh cloud, water-preserver your brightness is like dark Gopimohan (God Krishna). In addition, when you will come down into water of river, then sky wanderer sidhas looking down will see as if a beautiful bunch of necklaces of pearl is oscillating around neck of mother and in the middle a big blue bright gem is shining. Sky wanderer will see you without looking elsewhere. Is it less fortunate?

Stanza 47
Cloud!

Crossing the river Champavati proceed straight to north. On the way you will come across Daaspur city; beautiful women of that city will stare at your nice dark cloud. Is there any parallel to beauty of their eyes? Their eyes are beautiful; their glare is more beautiful with sweet gestures. When they will look at you raising their eyes, their eye-lids will be dancing artistically, it seems, as if, white colour is exposed from eyes and bubble bees are running in flocks. You will think that some white Kumud flowers have been thrown up by someone and black bubble bees are running from behind. You hold your attractive face before charming eyes of such beautiful women. And let them see.

Brother! Let them see their "pratickurban". Only they will see on the contrary, for seeing them by you do not delay further.

Stanza 48
Brother!

Then as you go on your way the land of Bramavarta will be seen. You also know the land is situated between the rivers, Saraswati and Dashaswati and it is the original abode of the Aryan people of India. You will move straight over the land. Land of Aryavarta, suffered from summer's heat will get cooled for a while from reflection of your cooling shadow and you will attend piety. Then on the way, you will come across Kurukshetra, the fierce battlefield between the Kauravas and Pandavas, where wounds of the Khatriya fighters' battle-bones of the fighters are still lying. Those will float in front of your eyes. Brother, as your discharge innumerable streams of water on blossomed lotuses and destroys those lotuses likewise, the great archer Dhananjay, on the battle field discharged three hundreds and thousands arrows at the faces of Kshatriya.

Stanza 49
Cloud!

In the most destructive war in India between the Kauravas and Pandavas, large-hearted, holder of divine plough, Baldev (elder brother of God Krishna) not joining any side in the battle out of sympathy, in feeling of separation in mind, sat on the shore of the river and concentrated on yoga. His better-half Revati went there thinking if she can take back her husband by bringing Baldev's favourite wine in her own hand and holding before the face of Baldev. Revati's loose but attractive eyes were being reflected on the pot of wine. Brother think how the wine is! Baldev did not look at wine, he went to that river ignoring pot of wine. That river, swaraswati will come before you. You, friend if you drink some water of such virtuous river, surely, I am telling you, your inside will be pure and stainless, only your outside colour will remain black.

Cloud!

From Kurukshetra you will have to go to Kankhal. "Prajapati temple" Dakshin sthan (or South place), "Satikundu" are various religious places by these names. Hearing vilification of husband by father, Daksha, daughter, Sathi breathed her last at this place-its name is "Satikundu". King, Daksha's yagnasthan.

Two miles west of this Kankhal, coming to Haridwar, Ganga has descended from the mountain. At the confluence of Ganga and blue streams this Kankhal is situated. Almost from the height of twenty two to twenty three thousand feet, coming down step by step along the slopes of the Himalaya, Ganga has descended on the plains at Haridwar. The gushing water of Ganga looks very nice. From the high places streams are falling and thick foams are being deposited every side.

Cloud! Looking down from the distant sky it will seem to you, as if, sons of king Saagar had gone to heaven climbing ladder through holy water of this Bhagirathi (Ganga); how many years ago they had gone, but those steps along the body of Himalayas are remaining till now. Singing ballads of famous Bhagirathi, brother cloud, you will know that, divine water pot of Brahma gradually coming down as Ganga from matted hair of Shiva fell on the surface of soil at Haridwar, five hundred feet above sea-level. You will further know that colour of foam is white as is the colour of laughing. Along the body of the mountain, on the slopes of stones, Ganga fell, formed condensed innumerable rows of foam. It will seem to you on looking, as if the two sides of those ditches through which streams of water is flowing down, are lips of mouth Ganga and rows of foam will resemble laughter of Ganga. Ganga is laughing loudly, raising above, hands are drawing matted hair of husband god Shiva, and Gouri Devi, another wife of God Shiva is looking with anger. You see, from Brahma's divine water-pot to matted hair of Mahadev and from there, going down step by step along body of mountains, Ganga has come downs to the plains. It seems that, at Haridwar Ganga Devi is dressing up properly, subsequently stretching her hands, pulling Mahadev with his matted hair. Devi's hand resembling waves, is also trying to catch moon of Chandrasekhar's forehead. The beams of unstained moonlight coming down from forehead of Chandrashekhar is mixing with the waves of Ganga. How wonderful that scenic beauty is. Cloud! At least once, from the distant sky, look at this unique image again and again. Your life will be blessed.

Stanza51
Cloud!

In the sky, in every direction so many elephants roam, they are called "Diggaj". Gods sitting on those elephants sometimes wander in the sky. Those elephants stretching long trunks draw water of trifala which is combination of three fruits (haritaki, amla and bahora) and drink.

Brother!

You also look like elephant. Such oily, black colour and stature of your body. You look like one of the God's elephants as you draw water from rivers and rivulets and release the water like a pillar of smoke. Brother as you float in the sky and stretching you become ready to drink unstained crystal-clear holy water coming from the chasm of the mountain, your dark shadow will reflect on crystal clear water of Ganga creating a beautiful picture. This play of colours will be seen in another place called Tribeni where Ganga-Jamuna have mixed with each other, Ganga's stainless and white flow being decorated with Jamuna's blue water. It is looking so beautiful.

Stanza52
Cloud!

As you are going and enjoying beauty, you will climb through the Himachal. Amongst mountains, it is the king, "Nagadhiraj", the originating place of "Patit-Paban" Ganga. Patit-paban Ganga means, if anybody takes bath in the water of Ganga his sins are removed. Crores of people across India believe in their hearts. It is the origin of Ganga. Mother Ganga arises at the origin from the foot of Vishnu and travels to divine water-pot of Brahma to matted hair of Dhujati, and from there along the peak of the Himalaya is leaping along the slopes of the mountain. Himalaya is considered as father. Brother! Has there any parallel to it? Here and there in the mountain, hordes of musk deer's coming sit on the icy-cold pieces of stones, lie down or welter around. Smell of musk from their belly-bottom spreads all over the mountain. Cloud! When you will sit on the covered ice peak of the king of mountain it will seem, as if, Trilachan Brishav Dharaj's large white ox is playing into soft soil by its horn and lump of wet, black soil is attached at its horn.

Stanza53
Brother,

On that Himalaya many forests of Devdaru trees can be seen. They have risen so high as if piercing through the sky are standing straight. At any point there is no bending, so their names are called Saraldrum. Branches are rubbing with each other making murmuring sound on the snow-covered mountain. Those Devdaru trees are thrashing fat branches with each other. Gradually from friction of the branches, fire broke out and wildfire spreads. The forests are burning and those sparks of fire floating in wind are falling on brushes of tails of chamari deers causing them burnt. Without any delay discharge rains in thousands at on spell and terrible fire will be extinguished. Chamri deers will be saved and surface of mountain will also get relief. Brother, do not hesitate at this critical moment. Those, who are really great, spend their wealth generously for the suffered. Successes come in such activity.

Stanza54

On the Himalayas, there are certain categories of deers which have eight legs; they wander and jump around day and night. You will not obstruct their path, but if they try to jump on you out of anger allow them to do so, since they cannot jump over you since their hands and legs will be smashed falling on stones of mountain. As they are naughty, teach a sort of lesson by discharging rain with thunder, and put them to immense trouble. Brother, not to speak of them but if anyone who tries to jump over others without any cause should be reprimanded.

Stanza55
Brother,

The Himalayas have footprint of God Shiva; nowhere exists such distinct print of God Shiva. You will see, many Siddha Deb yogis are always worshipping that footprint with various items. Siddha male or female, anybody may achieve their desire through practising yoga or any other method to achieve blessings of God or Siddhi.

Cloud, you move around that footprint with devotion of your heart after landing there. You will achieve immense blessings, those who sees footprint with respectful heart their sins are removed, and after death they achieve the status of first amongst equals of companion of lord Shiva. Be aware, do not miss this precious opportunity.

Stanza56
Brother, cloud,

Rejoice prevails all the time near the lotus like feet of Mahadava. Tall and thick bamboos on the mountain have got many pores, eaten by worms. The wind is entering into those pores, and it seems that thousands of flutes are playing sweet music. Well-dressed divine goddesses of heaven are singing beautiful songs narrating conquest of Tripur by Tripurari, God-Shiva. That time, if you sound low thunder and call up, the sound will reach caves of mountain and will echo like beating drums in hundreds and thousands. It will create divine situation for worshiping God Shiva with songs of Goddess of heaven, Kichak's music of flute from bamboos and your sound of thunder. The combination of three different performances will reach the highest stage of divinity which is beyond any materialist feeling.

Stanza57
Cloud!

You cannot proceed straight, seeing only those remarkable places on the slopes of the Himalaya's. In front of you Garalamandhata, not so high mountain, part of the Himalaya's will come on your way. Having full water in your body, you have to face trouble to cross that mountain. It is better to move through the tunnel and reach the other-end avoiding jumping over the hill, Garalamandhata. Do you know what the tunnel signifies? The brave Parshuram made the tunnel sticking series of arrows only. Subsequently, this tunnel has been known as grand chord for travelling from India to Tibet. You have to move through that tunnel. But brother you are unable to move that way being heavy with full of water. The tunnel has gradually gone up and then come out on the other sides; likewise, you have to also follow that step stretching your body. Now you think how you will be looking from amassed cloud stretching gradually like a pillion of cloud slowly rising above and going up bending depending on tunnel's size. It will be compared with the event of God Vishnu obstructing the path of king Bali, who is desiring to reach heaven, by deceiving king Bali camouflaging as a dwarf and raising and bending his small leg above which would turn to a thin new dark leg that grew longer and longer. Cloud! You will almost look like that.

Do not think it is a mere tunnel? It is a glorious achievement of Parshuram, son of Vrigunandan. Parshuram at the time of rising to heaven was opposed by that mountain and piercing through that mountain, he reached the heaven. It is no lesser feat.

Stanza58
Brother cloud,

As soon as you come up through this tunnel, in front of you will see a glass mountain Kailash covered with white ice. It remains covered with ice round the year. It seems the peaks are touching the sky covered with dust of white chalk.

Cloud! Coming to that Kailash Mountain, you will see, without the need of any looking glass, the faces of beautiful women from heaven.

On the way to Kailash, Ravan, brother of Kuber, king of Kailash had shaken the mountain with his twenty hands and since then joints of the slopes of the hill had been loose, resulting in white cracks on the slopes of the hill. God and Godesses of heaven enjoy themselves in great pleasure in those chasms. Brother, the mountain is standing around the sky with its thousand peaks covered with white ice. It seems the owner of Kailash, Nataraj Shiva laughs loudly every day and laughter gets condensed and remain in the sky in the form of white peak. Your eyes will be soothing.

Stanza59

Cloud, your colour reflects the colour of black collyrium. Do you know the colour of Kailash which is covered with ice? When the tusk of elephant is chopped and subsequently a piece of it is split again, the inside of it looks more white. When your black body floats on the edge of the mountain, it will seem that dark stole has been placed on the large body and broad shoulder of Balaram (elder brother of God Krishna). How beautiful your image will be? All the creatures moving on land and moving in sky will look at you gleefully. Seeing that beauty, they will be looking at you.

Stanza60

Kailash Mountain is the playing field of Hara Gouri (God Shiva and wife); this is the hilly-ground for their playing, walking and merriment. Going there you may also see God Shiva is wandering on foot holding hands of Gouri; being afraid of Gouri, throwing from his hands bangle of snakes, Mountain has so many places decorated with gems, inlaid with jewels. God Shiva extends hand to lift Parbati. If you see that scene without losing a fraction of moment, you place your body full of rain water like ladder before Hara-Gouri, father and mother of universe, and they will ascend easily placing their legs on the stairs of cloud. Brother! Your life will be successful. Your mind will be holy.

Stanza61
Brother!

You have to face some troubles. The women of heaven bejewelled with ornaments are wandering, running, playing and frisking, and creating holes in your body by bangles. Through those holes water will fall in thousands streams. It seems that water is falling from shower bath after many days of suffering from heat of sun. I am so unfortunate that perhaps your delay will be much longer there. Friend, if you think that this is no easy way to get released then you roar with terrible thunder. Their ears will be defunct and good senses will prevail upon them. By playing, they have only teased you, they have no ill motive; with your loud thunder their fun will come to end. In fear their thousand hands will go away. I am telling you your thunder is enough. Do not act more.

Stanza62

At this place, Kailash is situated. Manas-Sarovar is the only holy lake in Trilok (Swarga, Marta and Patal) where golden lotuses blossom in lakhs and lakhs. The famous elephant, "Oirabat" of Debaraj Indra likes to come here to drink water scented with pollen of golden lotus. You will at first drink some water of that Dev Sarovor and feel inside your body. Afterwards, if you come across that "Oirabat" elephant, you will be extending thin and broad parts of your body which is full of water and shower on the face of the elephant. The "Oirabat" will feel as if a piece of wet cloth got pasted on the face. Then "Oirabat" will happily thrash leaves of Kalpataru as wind blows those leaves.

Cloud, in this way you enjoy the king of mountain.

Kalpataru tree is that tree infront of which whoever or whatever wishes that wish gets fulfilled.

Brother that is place of enjoyment.

Stanza63

Brother! Where I am sending you on the lap of large snow-capped Kailash, the place is that Alakapuri of this unfortunate man. You are self-willed, when and where you want to go, you do that. Do you have any new thought? As you look you will understand that a beautiful city like Alakapuri cannot be simply built; along that city on the chest of mountain, Ganga is flowing making sweet sound. On the high slopes of the mountain, hither and thither, houses have been built in irregular manner. When you go up higher, you will see as if heroine is lying on the lap of her beloved, sleeping without sense under attractive cloth across her body. The cloth is detached from some parts of the body but is still attached under the body of pleasure loving women. Above the slopes of high mountain thick black clouds form and innumerable bubbles, streams of rivers roll down. It will seem to you, as if those lazy companions have not properly combed hairs and kept braids of hairs loose by removing net of pearls. Women like to wear pearls on red hairs.

Part 2

Meghdootam
Cloud On The North

Stanza 1
Cloud!

You will see at Alaka high rise buildings almost equally high like you.
You have lightning within yourself. Similarly, many beautiful women are
lightning up cottages of the palace; they are wandering everywhere. As
you have magnificent rainbow of different colours, those buildings are
also decorated with albums of colourful pictures hanging from the walls.
You have water in your body, rooms of those palaces are inlaid with
jewel and precious stone reflecting in such a way that water is flowing
abundantly. You are very tall. Alaka's palaces are also touching sky, it
seems, as if they are touching you.

Stanza 2
Cloud,

How much shall I tell you about beauty of my Alaka! Six seasons
prevail there all at a time. Flowers of six seasons blossom simultaneously.
Wives of Alaka, dressed with flowers will give pleasure to your eye.
You will see lotuses are always in their hands. When they move their
hands, lotuses also move. From black, long thrash of hairs bunch of
kumud flowers are hanging. Their faces become completely white with
pollens of stainless white lodhra flowers. Their faces are not rough and
dry in winter from the rubbing of lodhra flowers. From the braids of
hairs are hanging kurubak flowers. These kurubak flowers are newly
blossomed, their white thin leaves are swimming like black bubble bees.
How wonderful the picture is! The sirish- flowers spread fragrance
throughout. They get excited with fragrance of sirish-flowers. They
have tied a bunch of kadam flowers on either sides of the forehead
parting hairs. It is a beauty to enjoy! Meeting those women decorated
with six variations of flowers of six seasons, your pain and trouble will
be removed. Enjoying lotuses of sharat season, kunda flowers of
hemanta season, kurubak flowers of basanta season, shirish flowers of

summer season, kadamba flowers of rainy season, blossom all at a time. When you will see, your eyes will be mesmerized.

Stanza3
Brother,

Is there any parallel to that of Alaka? Flowers blossom all the time. Honey bees are fond of honey; fly around those trees, murmuring for sucking honey. It seems beautiful women are dressed with ornamented girdle of neckless, and sweet sounds of those ornaments can be heard. Domestic peacock's shoulder is always glittering from thousand moon light. They are not waiting for rains to come. All the time sounds of keka can be heard throughout the sky. Evening is charming, there is no trace of darkness as always, the moonlight is reflected.

Stanza4

Struck by Madan's (God of desire) arrow of flowers, the lovers have to suffer pains. They all are immortal, but still when desire strikes anyone, they cannot escape the love. This place is such that the age remains still.

Cloud!

Evening of Alaka, my birth place, is unique and magnificent in all respects. You will see there is only joy, no trace of sorrow and no one has shed tears of unhappiness. Lovers suffer from unhappiness being unsuccessful in love.

Stanza5
Brother cloud!

You will see at Alaka innumerable flowers of different colours scattered on cottages constructed with white and stainless moonstones. Inside the palace it seems that countless stars are glittering on the floor in those wonderful cottages, and Yakshas are drinking honey with beautiful young women around. Brother, this honey is not drawn from ordinary flowers, but collected from flowers of dream trees (Kalpataru); no other wine is better than this honey. Drinking such honey gives immense pleasure. Whoever tastes that honey, he is never averse to that taste. Your pleasant deep sound reaches that lovely intoxicated land.

Stanza6
Cloud!

Your eyes will be refreshed when you will look at river, Mandakini flowing on the gravel laden sandy path along the side of Alaka. You will even see, Gods become eager to take possession of those beautiful daughters of Yakshas. Those daughters of Yakshas are now playing and running on the strip of sandy land glittering like gold dusts, singing "searching searching nothing found, who will be picking, will be on pound". Yet they are not tired, because chilly wind of Mandakini is spraying water on them. On the shore under the shadow of Mander tree, heat of sun is lessened. So, you are going to the land of dream, just thinking of it, comes happiness.

Stanza7

In many places, there are customs to tie cloth around the waist; beautiful women of Alaka also tie clothes in that fashion. Their lips are reddish and glossy; their lovers with restless heart open clothes of women and begin to steal clothes. Thinking worst, women are perplexed and throwing sand put out the lamp to save from chastity. But the lamp refused to be extinguished as it is not the simple oil lamp, it is the scintillating light of the ornaments, so beautiful, women were defeated.

Stanza8

Alaka has many high-rise buildings with decorated rooms; beautiful pictures hang from the wall. Small groups of cloud enter through open windows and come out through the other side, as if, smoke from the fire place is coming out of the window. Clouds with full of water enter rooms and spoil the beautiful pictures as they cross touching them. Upon seeing this you will be crying in shame. Out of fear of being caught the clouds with fearful heart are fleeing. Such clouds are also like you. Be careful, do not do that unfair work. Do not enter into rooms of others, if you dare, your life will end on running, you will be unable to perform my task given to you.

Stanza9

What more shall I talk about pleasure and treasure of Alaka? I have already told you that. No such parallel exists in Trilok (Swarga, Marta and Patal). Inside the cottages, there are rooms for coition with beautiful beds under nice frilled canopies of moonstones hanging. Every tassel of the canopy gets illuminated under the moonlight. Now, you can imagine how beautiful the scene is. At night, when you distance yourself from the moon, then stainless moonlight, free from cloud, enters through window and touches every frill of moonstones. Owing to perspiration cold water falls in small drops. Under the canopy on the soft cot women being tired of coition under pressure of virile power of lovers are sleeping peacefully within the strong hands of males. Gradually, hands of lovers become loose. Moreover, cold water from moonstones is falling in small drops on their bodies. As a result, dirt is getting removed from the body of women, tiredness from coition at night is going away. Their bodies are looking fresh.

Stanza10
Cloud!

Imagine a place where the residents have no need to work or worry about earning a living. In the land of Alalka, there is a vast treasure of gold, jewels and precious metals, more than enough to last a lifetime. Instead of laboring, the people of Alaka spend their days enjoying the pleasures of life, such as visiting the garden known as Bhoiraj Choitrarath outside kuber bhavan. In this paradise, male residents can interact with fairies and listen to the melodic music of the celestial musicians as they tell tales of the deeds of the ruler Alaka. It is a place of endless beauty and enjoyment.

Stanza11
Brother, cloud!

You will be astonished, as soon as you will hear description of the landing steps of the city of Alaka. In the morning, Sun-God smiles in such manner, as if road of Alaka also smiles with Him and discloses the hidden stories of the residents. Women are nicely dressed for their tryst with male lovers. They decorate their hairs with Mander flowers which fall on the ground as the women hurriedly run. The leaves painted with sandal wood fall off, the earrings of golden lotus get detached from their ears. Due to their swaying movements, necklaces fall off from their bodies. They cannot hide their secrets from Sun-God.

Stanza12

God Mahadeva (God Shiva) has a good relation with Kuber who is owner of Alaka. Chandrashekhar (God Shiva) cannot depart from Alaka due to Kuber's high reverence for him. Even God of amorous desire, Madan, cannot play tricks with him. But Madan's habits die hard. Once his plan was completely shattered when he tried to disturb Mahadeva when he was in yoga. Since then Madan, moves in Alaka with fear. He would avoid directions where Mahadeva was staying. Once Mahadeva raised bow only in such effect that Madan was destroyed to ashes. After lots of persuasion Madan regained his life. His body was gone but body less Madan was taught a lesson to some extent. But who is doing this work? On whose influence women of Alaka are running to the secret place to meet their lovers? Madan's bow of flowers, arrows made out of Aravind, Ashok, Shirish trees are not effective in Alaka. It is the humorous women who are trapping their male lovers through their mischievous gestures of eyes.

Stanza13

In the land of Alaka, all desires are eventually fulfilled, although there may be a slight delay in granting them. The mythological wishing tree is extremely generous and will provide beautiful women with clothing and other luxurious items when they pray for them beneath its branches. The wishing tree supplies all types of items like eye-pleasing fabrics painted with swans, delicious wine that produces colorful images when drunk in moderation, fresh flowers and small plants and ornaments, and lac-dyed garments suitable for beautiful legs. All of these items are supplied by the generous wishing tree of Alaka. Cloud you imagine the splendor of my glorious homeland Alaka.

Stanza14

You need not search for long for my abode which is situated to the north of palace of king Kuber. From far away you will see gate of my residence as nice as rainbow which will be a pleasure for your eyes. I am giving you another sign for detection. Hear me! You will see from above a small Mandar tree inside the wall of the house, this is my residence. My beloved wife in her own hand has brought up the tree, which is now bent down from the weight of small new leaves. One can touch the leaves also. My beloved wife looks after the tree like her own son with affection.

Stanza15
Brother,

You will see further, there is a large pond inside my residence. The stairs leading down to the pond are adorned with green stones, and the water is filled with golden lotuses in bloom. The stalks of golden lotuses are adorned with blue vaidyaraj jewels. It is truly a stunning sight to behold. Drakes are so fond of that large pond that they have made this place their home. They never proceed to Manas Sarovar which is not far away from my residence, in spite of braving thousand rainy seasons. Going for pilgrimage to Manas Saravor in rainy season is a part of religion but having attraction to my lake they have rejected their religion.

Stanza16

Along the shore of that pond, you will find a small playing ground where I along with my better-half played number of games. The peak of the mountain is inlaid with rough indranil jewel and surrounded by gold banana trees. Cloud! You think of beauty of the mountain! That mountain is my wife's favourite. She has deep love for the mountain.

As you flash the lightning like creepers, the image of playing field on the mountain flashes in my mind. I look at you with a mix of pain and memories. It is true that seeing similar events from the past can bring pleasure, but it can bring a feeling of emptiness and fear.

Stanza17

Near the playing ground on the mountain inside the grove Madhabilata grows. Kurubak trees surround this Madhabilata tree. Near that grove two trees Ashok and Bakul grow. Leaves of Ashok tree with red flowers are oscillating in soft wind. It seems as if they are demanding something with folded hands from someone, which cannot be expressed in language. It seems they are communicating prayer from their heart. Brother, it seems Ashok tree is begging for onslaught by left leg of my wife, and another Bakul tree like me is communicating prayer for wine. My wife already drank and spitted some of it from her mouth.

You know, there is a practice, women with good fortune hit Ashok tree by left leg and spray mouthful water on Bakul tree to encourage the flowers to blossom. Even the famous actor's heart would not remain unamused in the off-season if they were to do this. The dry heart would blossom with various flowers of various desires.

Stanza18
Brother,

Among the two trees you will see the main root which looks like a golden stick buried in soil as if from the heap of a green jewel the crystal rod has come up. You will not find such beautiful similarity anywhere. Slowly afternoon is approaching. The blue necked peacock sits on the golden stick. My beloved wife encourages the peacock to dance by clapping and moving around peacock. The peacock also responses and dances in rhythm moving its blue neck. The ringing sound of bejewelled bangles of my wife makes the place dream like.

Brother, I am reminiscing one by one in my mind, this is exciting me.

Stanza19
Brother,

You are a saintly man and I am confident you will not forget my instructions. You will locate my residence looking at symbols I have told you about. In addition, there are images of one conch and one lotus painted on either side of the lion gate at my residence. Why painted do you know? At our Alaka, there is no man without wealth. How much wealth, anybody is in possession is written on the gate. For the curse, given by wealthy Kuber, I have fallen in distress today, otherwise, I am also owner of such quantity of wealth. One conch and one lotus mean I am in possession of one crore, arbud, kharba, nikharba. I am in possession of wealth in these numerical numbers of conch and lotus. You will locate my residence seeing these signs. But my residence may have lost its beauty, glamour and glitter. In my absence, not only my wife even beautiful palace has lost its glory. Cloud! If sun sets can the lotus retain previous beauty?

Stanza20
Cloud,

Can you remember I have told you of the playing ground on the mountain and about its charm near my residence? Cloud, you will need to shrink your body down to the size of a small elephant in order to sit on the sparkling waist of the mountain. There won't be any difficulty for you, but you must be careful as you descend onto the mountain's waist. Once you are seated on the mountain's slopes, release the lightning inside of you slowly, allowing it to enter into my room through the window at a slow pace as well. Be careful not to disturb anybody in the room with your intense lightning and search through the dim light carefully like fireflies.

Brother, when fireflies gather and burn brightly on trees, you will also be able to see your own lightning in your eyes.

Stanza21

In my mind I can see the thin body, the beauty of your teeth, the attractive ripen bell fruit like lips. The thin waist moves like trembling deer. The belly is deep like Sarovar and unable to walk fast. The body is slightly bent. God who thinks alike creates such beauty in women's world.

Stanza22
Cloud,

In the room you will see someone is lying. The most beautiful woman is wife of this ill-fated man. She is like my second life. She does not talk much without any necessity. Her only companion is me. I am spending days at the distant place, Ramgiri. As Chakrabuki (female bird) becomes restless loosing Chakrabuck (male bird), my beloved wife also is suffering in such way. She is now, perhaps silent and lying without movement. She is still a girl. What will be her age? She is only sweet sixteen. Long separation from me is unbearable to her. In my absence, her sorrow has increased hundred times. It seems that glamour of her beautiful youth is no more and has become pale from unbearable separation. Her beauty is comparable to the lotus being thrashed by snow.

Stanza23

Tears roll unstopped,

Eyes are always full of tears,

Swollen for weeping,

Eyes are not bright.

Long breathing is frequent,

Flowing without break.

Red-colour lips became pale,

Covered with long hairs,

Kept under left palm.

Unexpressed her pain of face.

Cloud, right you are

Cover the sky with your shadow,

Removed stain of moon.

Stanza24
Oh, cloud!

Perhaps you will see my wife busy performing various rituals for worshiping Goddess for my welfare. I have been banished to faraway place. She is thinking about our long separation and how my health be. She is painting my image in her mind or she is asking sarika (parable bird, confined within cage) about my whereabouts and its feelings. She will ask, "my Sarika do you remember how you used to show humorous gestures to my husband? He used to love you. Like me, does your heart burn? Tell me truly". In this way my wife is spending days alone in the vast palace without any companion.

Stanza25
Oh! Calm image, cloud!

I am understanding your gestures. You go there, no need to fear, you look for my wife. You will find her singing keeping Veena on her lap. Brother, reminiscing it, my heart breaks. I cannot remember when I left her; she has also left her all dresses and valuable wealth. She is spending days wearing one dirty cloth, keeping Veena on the support structure covered by dirty cloth. She is trying to sing songs maintaining tunes in rhythm, but she is unable to sing. She has composed song in my name and with words spoken by me. She wished she will sing that song in solitude playing strings of Veena. As soon as she is going to tune Veena's strings, it became wet with tears from eyes, strings of Veena go out of tunes. Realizing she quickly erased tears but could not sing. My wife has forgotten the song which she herself composed and tried to recall again and again. Cloud, think of her mental condition.

Stanza26
Brother,

When you go there you may see my beloved wife in the corner of the door from where I left her one year back bidding goodbye to her. From that day she has placed a flower there every day and in eight months a total of two hundred twenty four flowers have accumulated. She counts them one by one by one keeping those flowers on ground and wonders how many more days of separation are left before this suffering ends. You will see her bending her body on the boundary wall and closing tired eyes thinking deeply about life within life and life itself.

Brother, in that solitary palace although my wife remains alone, during day time she gets busy with work to lessen her pain willingly or unwillingly from this separation. But at night when I think of her, I am afraid of my life. At that time, she cannot avoid the pain. I do not know, how much pain your companion feels, she spends whole night without sleeping! She lies on the bed of dust. None to take care of her. She is a woman of chaste in my life without me; she is thinking in imaginary mind, she is immersed in herself, having devoid of external sense.

Brother, cloud!

Thinking about that I go out of mind and I start talking too much. Friend, it is not all about that. You will see that women cherish their lives in other ways once she loses her companion. Cloud, when you will go there, you will see that my presumption is right or wrong.

Stanza27
Cloud!

In that solitary palace, she is staying alone. During day time she gets busy with work to lessen her pain willingly or unwillingly from this separation. But when I think of night, my life shivers from fear. There is no way to distract her mind. I do not know how much she is suffering whether the whole night she spends without sleeping or trying to sleep a little on the ground in the dust. There is no one to take care of her. She is very chaste and has unblemished character. You do not pass on information about me to her during day time. You convey message or have a glance at my wife at night when the whole world is silent and sleeping and my wife is lying on ground in dust with anxiety like pigeon being struck by arrows.

Stanza 28

Cloud!

You will see her lying on one side of bed on scattered dusts. Is she alive now? She has become very from the pain she is suffering from separation. Looking at her fear engulfs in mind. I understand, there is not much time left to the life. New moonlight appears in the horizon of the east at the end of fourteen nights. Likewise, you will see new moon coming at the end of the night. My heart rejoices at the thought of the new moon coming. So, you do not delay; go fast, convey message to her and save her life. Cloud, during our good old days, we happily spent time together. On that night of union of our hearts both of us had immense pleasure and enjoyment. How quickly the night ended. Now we are separated, myself staying on the hill and she in the solitary palace. I still enjoy that night of happiness in my mind even though the romance has ended in our life.

She is spending the long nights of separation weeping, warm tears of eyes are rolling down from two cheeks and my beloved wife is lying on one side of bed like bunch of grasses.

Stanza 29

The pain in my heart has not abated at all and my mind is not at peace. How will my distressed wife survive? Tell me. Through the window moonlight has entered. Alas, one day this light was so pleasant and we were happy. It relieved our fatigue and tiredness but after becoming tired from our intimacy, my beloved wife fell asleep and her body and mind were refreshed. Today, in this distressed time of unbearable separation, I understand that the moonlight of our two hearts will cool our minds and bring joy to our eyes. Thinking this, my wife, distressed from separation, looked at the moonlight coming through the window with great hope and her eyes shone. But then, quickly closing her eyes, my miserable wife tried to find relief from this new pain, but could not keep them close for long. Can tearful eyes be closed? Then her lotus like long eyes remained neither open, nor closed, seemingly suspended in this position like a lotus on a cloudy day that neither blooms nor remains a bud.

Stanza30
Cloud,

Or you will perhaps see, my beloved wife is trying her best to sleep hoping she may see me in dream. Because after awakening she cannot see me. But she cannot close tearful eyes. So she remains lying on bed with the thoughts of reunion of her heart. Tears of eyes are rolling down along her two cheeks as she is reminiscing, her hairs are pasted with tears coming from cheeks. Warm breath dries up the tears on the soft cheeks. She does not oil her hair nor does she take bath and hairs become thin. She did not sleep from the very first day of separation. Those women who have been separated from companion, do not oil hair or dress up. For whom will they comb? Brother, eventually the beauty goes, the thin hairs parted on either side of the forehead fly in wet wind and fall on the cheeks. You will see her lying on unclean bed without any companion.

Stanza31
Brother!

Dry hairs that have fallen on her neck are always swinging, and hairs fly with each breath she takes. She is feeling uneasy. You think once. Moreover, when I left her that was first day of separation, her hairs have been braided with a plate. Separated women are not permitted by custom to braid hairs by more than one bunch. Braid of hairs was decorated with garland of beautiful flowers; those have been thrown out. Now braid of hairs is hanging like a rounded mass. There is no way to open that hair of round mass. After my banishment when I shall return, I shall open that braid of hairs with my own hands. With this thought she does not open her braid of hairs. The thin dry hairs give pain to her and there is itching in her head; yet she is unable to give relief by her own hand as she has long nails which she cannot cut due to separation. Cloud! You think of her pain. What a mental and physical pain she is going through.

Stanza32
Cloud!

You will see, there is not a single ornament on her body. The golden colour of her body becomes dark. She is unable to bear her body weight and lying on bed. I feel sad when I think of that. When you will see, I do not know, how grief will engulf you. How painful will be your mind.

Oh, new cloud, when you will see her, surely tears will roll down from your eyes, like releasing your new drop of water. You cannot remain quiet; you will also weep. You are full of water which will melt down in grief.

Stanza33
Brother!

The deplorable condition of her life from separation has made her sober. No one would understand the deep love between husband and wife.

Brother! Now I know of her deep and affectionate love towards me. I am not sharing this emotion with anyone, this is my secret. There is not much to tell you. You are already going to her, and you will see what I have told is true or not.

Stanza34
Cloud!

I can see through my divine eye, like Vidur narrating to blind Dhritarashtra from the war front in the battle between the Kauravas and the Pandavas in the epic Mahabharata, how my wife will look at you when you go to her. How her eyes will swing, how the image in the eyes will reflect when rough braid of hairs fall on the corner of her eyes, and how their beauty will shine. She will turn her eyes to look at you as you approach her, lying thinly on the bed, suffering from the pain of separation. Her eye lids will dance with rhythm. Brother, she has so beautiful eyes once I felt like drinking wine looking at those eyes. Today, time has changed. There is no black collyrium applied on the beautiful eyes anymore; the dry hairs are not in place and fall on the corner of the eyes. Even she does not drink wine, beauty of eyes has resultantly gone away, that usual bewilderment coupled with beauty of drowsiness wither away from my separation. She has abandoned all her habits – looking down, casting side long glances and observing through drowsiness.

Brother, the upper lids of her eyes are always distressed from fear like eyes of deer, slightly restless like the leaves of a lotus. You will think the stars inside her eyes are moving around as if fishes are swimming in blue water and the movement of the fish causes the leaves of the blossomed lotuses to sway.

Stanza35
Cloud!

My wife's left thigh will tremble when she will see you. Women recognize their dearest ones as soon as their left thigh trembles. So, my wise wife can now understand that she will see her husband very soon. Brother, that thigh has lost glamour during this long separation. There are no signs of wounds, caused by the strike of my nail; those wounds have long since dried. Previously, during our intimate moments, she used to wear frill of diamonds beneath her cloth around the waist. When the frill moved, it touched her thigh, she felt cold and shivered. I was in a happy mood. Today, my heart is broken, when I think that nice thigh of my wife, no longer, exists. Her thigh resembles banana tree when its bark is detached it looks white.

When she got tired after enjoying many ways of our beautiful moment, I would massage her loose senseless body. Her drowsiness used to get removed through my massage only.

Cloud!

Looking you as first ambassador of my dearest wife, her thigh will be trembling continuously.

Stanza36
Brother cloud,

That time, if you see that she is sleeping deeply, you will also wait and sit by her side carefully and silently. Do not get restless to roar immediately. At least wait for three hours. After she wakes up there is no end of sorrow; so, if she sleeps for a while, brother, do not interrupt. May be, in sleep she is looking at me. Through her dream she is embracing my neck firmly with her hands. Her sleep will be disturbed if you make noise. Her dream will get shattered and those hands which are embracing my neck will fall down. Then she will heave a long sigh. Brother, three hours' time is very insignificant, let her enjoy such imaginary embracing whish she is missing.

Stanza37
Brother,

As I have told you earlier, going there perhaps you will see she is sleeping. You will break her sleep very slowly taking proper care. Be careful, do not wake her sounding loudly and trembling across the sky. In the morning your cold wind with full water when touches, buds of Malati flowers are blossomed on their own, likewise, wind in the morning carrying your drops of cold water will touch her body.

Immediately her eyes will open. My wife will be looking without blink of her eyes at that window where you have taken seat. Brother, my wife will be bewildered suddenly looking at the black cloud. She has just woken up so cannot identify you at that time. So, my request, very slowly, you will start talking to her. If you do not behave in proper way, she will turn away her face in pain. You are not aware of that she is a very self-respected woman. If you cannot conceal your lightning inside of you, then she will not be able to look at your lightning flashes. That poor eyed woman, my wife, will turn her face. You are learned, calm and quiet. Friend, you know how to talk to an unknown distressed woman who lives at solitary palace without any companion. Gradually, making low sound you will begin talking to her.

Stanza38

At first you will tell, that you are her husband's intimate friend and address her as Abidhabe. She will at least know that her vermilion is still intact along her parting hair. As you tell her that you are friend of her husband, who is cursed by Kuber, water will flow in her life. Being assured, she will look at you, she will hear your words minutely. Do not stop, you will speak continuously. You bring hope in her heart with your first word. Tell her, "I am cloud, don't be frightened seeing me. My aim is to throw heat of world. I will also give you relief. I am a messenger of happy news of your husband. He has sent me to you to share many secret news. I have come here to present those words weaving in mind. I remove pain from those who all are burning from the fire of separation like you. I give life to them whose husbands are living at faraway places. When I appear the distressed women run quickly home and take long breathe after being tired from running. As I sound lowly in the sky, they feel happy at the advent of rainy season – feeling such romance, women in separation from their husbands run madly to unlock their braid of hairs, which were attached on the first day of separation."

Stanza39
Cloud,

As soon as you tell these words, "I am a friend of your husband," she will look at you raising her face. When Hanuman, sun of wind God (Pawan) told Sita, wife of Ramchandra in epic Ramayana, at Ashok forest whereabouts of God Ram, she adoringly looked at hanuman. Likewise, my wife will also look at you, her heart will flow with happiness till the brim. You are friend of her husband, you have gone to convey whereabouts of her husband, knowing this she will treat you as her guest with pleasure and she will hear your words with heart and soul.

Brother,

You already know, that to get this news of dearest husband who is staying far away is as good as enjoying those happiest moments of sharing emotions with the dearest husband.

Stanza40
Brother,

I wish you long life of hundred years who do a good job for others. You are going at my request to my dearest wife, who is in extreme pain from separation. If you fulfil my prayer you will also be benefitted on this mission. You are devoted to save two lives, is it a less fortunate job? How many people can perform this job? So, going to fulfilling my prayer, you are also getting chance in your life to succeed. Cloud, keeping in mind all these aspects, addresses her – "Frail woman! You have no strength in your heart, it is as soft as flowers. Your husband is alive and is staying faraway at Ramgiri Hills. He is thinking how you are bearing such separation from your life time companion. He made deluges when you were out of sight even for a moment and is now spending days with unbearable grief. He has left you long ago, he has not received any news of you. He has sent me to ask about your health".

Cloud!

You already know, danger one after another follows humans closely: living is a wonder but no wonder is in dying. So, at very first always you should greet saying "How are you" when you see someone.

Stanza41

"Today your physical condition and that of your husband's is same from unbearable pain of separation. My heart breaks as I look at him the way I look at you now. He is staying at faraway place and owing to misfortune all the ways leading to you are closed. Like you his body has also become weak and thin. As your body is burning day and night since eight months his mind is also burning from this separation. As the tears roll down from your cheeks, similarly, he also breaks down into tears. As you feel bad day and night for your husband, eager to see him at least once, his feeling is also same as he is thinking of you day and night. Yours and his breathing rhythm remains same. As you think of your husband, he is also thinking of you. Thinking about him your health deteriorated. Your husband understands you and in desperation wants to unite with you."

Stanza42

Tell her, "Please say something whatever you want to say." She will bend on your ears to say that her husband could not stay even for a moment. You will tell "Today unfortunately, your husband who is so loving and affectionate to you is staying at far distant place, his words do not reach you; but, your husband, distressed in separation, staying at faraway place, still thinks of you. I am an unknown person and I am compelled to tell you about his emotional words. Please hear me."

Stanza43
Cloud,

Hear me. I am compelled to tell you because you may be angry. I see your exceptional beauty, incomparable glamour of your face. I hope looking at your beauty my life will become pleasant. With this hope I have travelled like beggar. I have found no such beauty like you. You have concealed yourself so well you did not keep any of your sign in tribhuban (heaven earth and infernal world). I do not get any solace in my life. I run to priyangul creeper which oscillates in slow wind. I see your thin body like creeper with humorous gestures. I look at the trembling eyes of deer which resemble side glance of your restless eyes. I look at full moon for enjoyment of beauty of your face, even for a fraction to bring pleasures to my eyes. I look at the feathers of deer's tail to see your beauty. I look at the shrivelled hairs and your restless oscillating eyebrows. I look at your side glance which can make my life successful. I look at slow small waves on the shores without winking my wyes for some hope, but my heart breaks. Alas! I do not see any resemblance of any part of your body on any matter. You are so peerless, so nice.

Stanza44

Our love manifested when you became angry from my teasing. In anger your face, neck, eyes turned red and attracted me so much that I teased you more. I enjoy such happiness in mind. At the end, there was no way to lessen your anger and to soften your mood I fell on your feet. I would think how happy those days were. In this period of separation, I drew your lovely image on stone with red soil and I drew my image below your red feet thinking about union of our hearts. Although, physically union was not possible at least, in this way we could make physical union through image. But destiny has something different for me. I lose my eyesight; I cannot see anything. My cruel fate cannot tolerate our union of two hearts. Through my tears I can no longer draw my image under your feet. I start crying aloud.

Stanza 45

Sleep does not come easily to me. But I try my best to sleep hoping at least I can see you in dream, give me chance to see you. Sleep does not soothe me anymore. But I try to do everything to sleep so that I can find you in dream. In my dream I try to embrace you deeply, I raise my two hands high to touch you. I stay for a long time raising my hands. In the solitary forest, looking at my restless behaviour Gods of forest cry from sympathy. Their tears fall like diamond drops. Those places become ominous on which the tears fall. It is custom when seniors shed tears the women will erase with their loin cloth. Gods of forests also shed water from eyes on leaves of trees, these are their tears. But the general people do not understand and say these are dews.

Stanza 46

In rainy season moist cold wind is blowing from north which touches small buds of "Debdaru" tree. Gradually the leaves are unfurling and some leaves are getting detached. The white gum that is oozing out from the stalks of the leaves gets hardened quickly. Nice scent is spreading everywhere as rainy wind is blowing gleefully. Entire Ramgiri hills are maddened in such fragrance! Oh my dear wife! you have so many virtues, how shall I describe you? When you came to me or when you passed my body closely, then also, such fragrance of your body had maddened me. That wind is also coming from north. You remain around my whole world. Wherever you are wind brings your fragrance to me. Maybe that wind touched your scented body. So, I run to catch that cold wind to wrap my body, thinking in such way at least I can get you, I can meet you and enjoy with you.

Stanza 47

My dearest wife,

Day and night I am bearing same pain as yours. I cannot bear any more pain. I am reminiscing that you are giving me a glance through corners of your eyes rolling your eyeballs sidewise. I am in more distress looking at your glance and want to hold you. This desire has no end at this time of night. Now it is three quarters of night (prahar) – one quarter consists of seven and a half "danda" that is also a little time. Moreover, night is very small in summer and in rainy season night is too small; yet that one quarter of three quarters of night is like hundreds of years to me. I think how to decrease the duration of night, if I could pass the night within a twinkle of an eye. What about day? What more of my pain can I say? Sun on the hills turn my chest dry. My life becomes colourless. My body burns from inside and outside due to the pain from this separation as if it will turn into ashes. I think how the heat of day will come down, but who will listen to my prayer? It is whose responsibility? I am becoming restless from this separation from you. I cannot find solace wherever I go or whatever I do. Alas! Is here anybody who can lessen my pain, give me some shelter in this bad time? Oh my wife! Now I am shelter less, what more shall I tell?

Stanza 48

Thinking continuously I console myself that by any means if I spend a few months more, I shall be able to reach to you. At this thought I hold to my life. I bless you. You also make your mind strong. My graceful wife, my ever-deserving well-wisher, do not lose hope. You stay with patience a little bit. Who will pacify you if you become restless? Who will console you? My graceful wife sorrow does not remain forever. In this world, do you think that both happiness and sorrow stay permanently forever? In case of man, happiness and sorrow are like edge of a wheel, sometimes, happiness is up on the wheel and afterwards it goes down the wheel. Today, who has sorrow, tomorrow he has happiness, again, today who has happiness tomorrow he has sorrow. Remembering these words, you console your mind.

Stanza49

How long can I console myself! I think of you not to be any more restless, no more to wait. This is the month of ashad (rainy season); from now, four months later on the eleventh day of the bright fortnight, God Narayana will wake up leaving His last bed. On that day my curse will come to end. That is the first part of season sharat. The second part of the season sharat is wonderful, highly enjoyable. My dear wife, spend remaining four months anyhow, closing your eyes and ears, stay with patience. Keep on thinking that this is also happiness when cloudless moons reflect transparent light at night. When the good time comes both of us will have same good old moment of emotions and intimacy. We shall enjoy all of our desires. No desire will remain unfulfilled. I beg you, spend a few more months.

Stanza50

Brother, cloud! You may perhaps think that I am sending you but, she may not believe you. She may think you are trying to mislead her citing various relationships. Then what is the way out? So, I am sharing with you some information, which, except me, no one knows in the world. As soon as she hears this story, she will understand that truly you are her husband's intimate friend. Tell her that her husband has shared a secret with you. He has asked you to remember one incidence at night when you were sleeping deeply holding his hands you suddenly woke up crying. When your husband asked you what is the reason for crying, you laughed mischievously and replied, "characterless, just now I dreamt that you were enjoying with another woman."

Cloud, when she will hear this incident, she will not think you as a treacherous person.

Stanza51

Oh, my black-eyed wife! Today, at the time of sending my messenger cloud, I am remembering only your black eyes like bubble bee. Your every feature is beautiful, your beautiful two black eyes reflect image in your stainless moon like face. All these messages I sent to you, all private matters, no other knows except me. So, from this message you will understand that I am alive. I am staying at a faraway place for a long time. The unfortunate women and bad men say bad words about me. They will say I have been away for so long, so my previous sobriety must have gone astray. You do not listen to them, do not trust them. I am yours. I am not a man to betray you. Those who are not true lovers will lack in common sense and will believe in materialism only. They will say that in the heat of separation affection dries, like camphor it goes away, only pot remains. But in reality, it is opposite. In separation, whoever desires in true sense the love he becomes spiritualistic and performs prayer to God from heart. The true lover will think as if she is busy in stitching garland of various flowers plucking from garden of heart. From the separation, the love that has doubled into thousands of streams of deep love will flow down as hundreds of streams during the time of union. Have I to make my wife aware of this matter? No, my affection for my wife has not waned, I have not changed. The man of the heart's love still exists. Whenever anyone speaks otherwise, do not let it reach her ears. In enjoyment beauty fades but, in separation when enjoyment is not available beauty increases- it is a simple truth.

Stanza52
Brother cloud!

In her new life, she is detached from me by first strike which is unbearable. That image of my wife which I have cherished in mind will become restless. So, without any delay go to her and share the information; you save her and protect me. After conveying message to her, you immediately come down from the Kailash Mountain. Do not delay sitting there. That mountain is very rough. The dangerous bull of God, Shiva plays ousting all from the small peaks of the Mountain. He strikes with his horn so powerfully that hard stones get smashed. You will also sit across one of the peaks when you will go there. Can those who have horns stay aloof without striking you as soon as they see your soft body full of water? During day, if that bull finds you, there is no way to escape. He is the bull of God. When it becomes angry there is no way for protection, there is no legal provision to lodge complaint against misbehaviour of the bull. God Shiva has three eyes. Once God Madan played some tricks with God Shiva and he was burnt to ashes by His Third eye. So do not delay. You return back very quickly and when you will be coming, bring some memorabilia of my wife and tell me what she had replied to my messages.

Stanza53
Cloud!

In the morning, buds of kumud flowers get detached from their stalks under the wind and fall on the soil, likewise, I will also not survive as my life gets separated from my wife. Brother, you give me life bringing her message to me. She is still alive, knowing this I may survive with hope of union with her. I am looking to your path (way). Do not forget our life and death are now at your hands.

Oh! New cloud, oh! Ever nice one!

You have heard my prayer deeply and attentively. But have you agreed to the task given by your wretched friend? Have you agreed to go to my darling wife as a messenger? You have heard calmly my entire message, but did not reply and I am not feeling bad about it. I am not thinking ill of you that perhaps you have not agreed. On the contrary if you said "well I shall complete your task given by you" then I would have thought that you have become restless. I know that when thirsty, swift flying birds come singing to you for water you silently provide them with water without speaking any word. Those who are great, their dharma (religion) is in karma. They give reply to the prayers by completing the desired tasks for their friends. They do not give reply in words. So, in your silence, I am feeling pleasure. So I am understanding though you are not replying in words, you will reply surely through performance.

Stanza54

Brother! I have requested you in very unperceived way. You have to go to faraway place Alaka crossing so many mountains and hills, big rivers and rivulets, bushes and forests, different lands, is it easy job for you? But cloud! By any means complete my task bearing trouble whatever it may be. As you love me, in spite of me being in distress without any shelter and still showing your kindness to me at the moment if I may die soon being cursed by Kuber, I request you to complete my task given to you. Do not deprive me. After that you may go anywhere, you like. Now you are filled with beauty of new rain, you may wish to travel or wonder to new place but first complete my task given to you.

Cloud! I convey to you that I am grateful to you. I bless you from my heart and soul. I am praying that in your life, even for a moment you are not detached from your lightning. Today losing my lightning, moon of my life, my beloved wife, I have been distressed. Do not fall in danger, even for a moment, do not get separated from your lightning.

END.